CHRISTMAS
Craft Book
30 fun & festive projects to make with kids

CHRISTMAS
★ Craft Book ★
30 fun & festive projects to make with kids

Laura Minter & Tia Williams

Contents

Introduction

Christmas is such a special time for crafting. It's a time when items made years ago by tiny toddler hands are carefully unwrapped and hung up on the tree, bringing back happy memories. It is the perfect time of year to snuggle up and make some handmade items that you and your kids will treasure for years to come, along with the memories of making them together.

This book is crammed fuller than Santa's sack with projects to help you and your children create a memorable handcrafted Christmas. Each of the 30 makes comes with step-by-step instructions and accompanying photos, plus templates where required to help you along the way. There are quick, fun projects for children, such as the Penguin Party Poppers (see page 100) and the Quick Christmas Tree Decorations (see page 44) plus more elaborate ones, such as Santa's Elf (see page 58) and the Festive Wreath (see page 10) that you can make over several evenings, curled up with some hot chocolate. There are also some personalized ones, such as the advent calendar based on your home (see page 14) and the Pompom Stocking (see page 124) that allow you to make unique keepsakes for friends and family.

So, grab your materials, crank up the festive tunes and get Christmas crafting with us. It's Craftmas time!

Tools, Materials & Tips

Craft materials

It is likely that you will already have a lot of the materials you'll need for the projects in this book. Other items, such as the copper tubing for the Copper Star Light (see page 72) and the ring for the Festive Wreath (see page 10) can easily be bought online or from craft and DIY stores.

We recommend you have a flick through the projects well ahead of December, as some take a little time to make and you'll want others ready right at the start of the festive season. Mark the ones you want to make yourself and those that you want to do with the children, stock up on the materials, and set aside a rainy (or snowy!) day to get started on them.

These things are useful to have in stock:

- **Colored card, paper, tissue paper, and corrugated card:** these and a stash of old cardboard boxes of different sizes is always useful.
- **Paints:** child-friendly versions plus acrylic paint, for projects that need better coverage and durability.
- **Embellishments:** decorations such as pompoms, rickrack, string, ribbon, and googly eyes are fun to add.
- **Fabrics:** our favorite fabrics for making things with kids are felt and fleece as they don't fray. We also use cotton, corduroy, and velvety fabrics.
- **Yarn:** we love nothing better than a little collection of colorful wool to make pompoms and fairy hair!
- **Natural materials:** have a festive walk to collect twigs and pinecones for the Natural Decorations (see page 30).

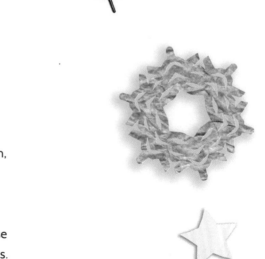

Crafting with Kids

We know it's not all twinkles and elf dust; crafting with kids can be stressful and short lived. Plus, when you add the stresses of the millions of other things you have to do at Christmas it can feel like a hassle you really don't need. We speak from experience. But, we have also found that setting aside time for making and baking (almost as though it is another chore that must be ticked off) can result in the most fun and memorable moments.

There have been many times we've dreading making things. We'd put it off until our kids made us feel guilty and we'd give in. And then, it would surprise us to find that we enjoy making things with them way more than we thought we would. So much so that when the kids have got bored and wandered off, we are still there, cutting, coloring, or drizzling icing. When you let it get to you, art can be very restorative.

The best way to reduce any stresses is to get all the materials prepped and ready in advance, cover all work surfaces, as well as yourselves and the kids, and devote time to it. Switch off your phone. Reduce the sharing squabbles by letting each child have their own little selection of paints or tools. Let your kids be in charge of what they are making by allowing them to choose their materials and colors. You can make your own version of whatever it is to give them some inspiration, but allowing them to take control reduces the likelihood that you will try to take over with theirs. And if the end results don't look exactly like they do on these pages then that's perfect as they're unique and personal, just like they should be.

Crafting Safely

Please bear in mind that all crafting with children should be done with supervision and sense. Most of the crafts in this book can be done at least in part by children with adult assistance. There are some tools that are of course not suitable for children to use, even with supervision. Craft knives, like the one used for the advent calendar, must only be used by an adult.

Of course it goes without saying (but we will still say it!) that projects involving an iron, glue gun, pruning clippers, or an oven must be done with care and common sense.

9

Festive Wreath

This beautiful felt wreath is a lovely Christmas make that will last for years to come. It's easy to make from felt and pipe cleaners. You could even add fairy lights if you wanted it to be a little twinkly! Metal hoops, often used for macramé, are available to buy from craft stores or online.

You will need

- 4 sheets of green felt, 9 x 12in (23 x 30cm), in different shades
- 1 sheet of red felt, 9 x 12in (23 x 30cm)
- Scissors
- PVA glue
- 8 pipe cleaners
- 12in (30cm) metal hoop
- A handful of black and multicolored pompoms
- Glue gun (optional)
- Pegs (optional)
- 12in (30cm) fishing wire (optional)

1 To make the stems, cut eight strips, roughly 1in (2.5cm) wide, from the length of the light and dark green felt. Paste PVA glue all down one side and wrap each one diagonally around a pipe cleaner. Repeat to make eight stems.

2 Roughly cut circles of different sizes (1–2in/2.5–5cm) from the remaining felt. You will need approximately 60 altogether, enough for seven or eight per stem. Cut three larger (about 3in/7.5cm wide) circles from red felt.

3 Add a dot of glue to a green circle of felt, near the edge. Pinch it together to make a leaf. A glue gun is good for this as it sticks instantly, but if you'd rather use PVA, you can use pegs to hold the leaves in position while the glue dries, working in batches.

4 Glue seven or eight leaves onto each stem.

5 Twist the stems onto the hoop, leaving a gap or covering the whole thing if you prefer. Glue down the ends of the stems.

6 Cut slits into the red felt circles to resemble flowers. Glue black pompoms to the middle of each one.

7 Glue the flowers onto the wreath, along with some pompoms.

8 Hang the wreath to a nail on your door, or use a length of fishing wire to tie it on.

Our House Advent Calendar

This is a lovely way to make yourself a personalized advent calendar that only you will have. It features your own house and pictures of your family and festive moments. You don't have to use photos of course, you could also draw pictures in, or cut out Christmassy images from magazines.

You will need

- 2 sheets of white card, about 12 x 16½in (30 x 42cm)
- Pencil
- Paint
- Paintbrushes
- Coloring pens
- Ruler
- Craft knife
- Masking or painter's tape
- Festive photos
- Scissors
- Craft glue

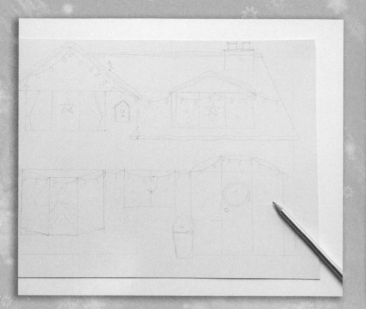

1 Start by getting outside and taking a good look at your house! Draw it or take pictures so you have a clear record of what it looks like. Then, on a piece of card, sketch out the house in pencil, so that it fills the page. You don't need to be too detailed at this stage.

2 Paint all the main parts of the house and background, making sure none of the paper is unpainted. Leave to dry.

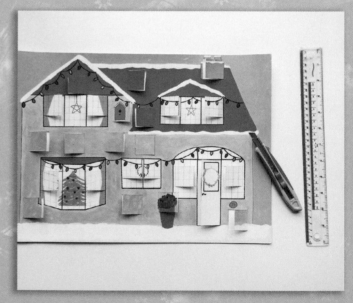

3 Add in the details of your house plus festive features using fine paintbrushes and coloring pens for any fiddly bits. Then mark out 24 squares measuring 1½in (4cm) in pencil. Make one a bit bigger for the final window. You could use the front door for this, or the chimney.

4 Ask an adult to use a craft knife to very carefully cut out the advent windows, making sure you leave one side attached for a hinge. Gently score along the hinge on the reverse of the picture with a blunt knife to create an even fold. Open up the windows.

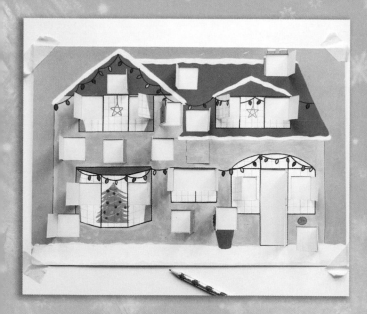

5 Place the calendar onto the other piece of card. Line the edges up carefully and tape it in position. Draw around each of the 24 windows onto the card underneath.

6 On your computer, find 24 festive photos and scale them each to 1½in (4cm) square. Find a special one for the last window and make it the right size. Print out the pictures, then cut them out and glue into the marked squares.

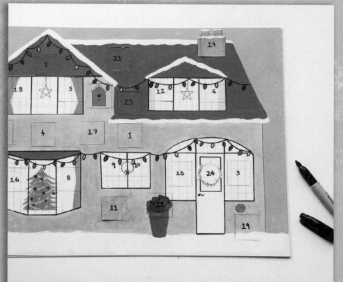

7 Close all the advent windows on your house picture. Add glue to everywhere on the other piece of card, apart from the pictures. Be careful not to spill any glue on them as you will glue your windows shut! Carefully line up the house picture on top of the pictures card and glue the two pieces together. Leave under a tray with heavy books on it while the glue dries.

8 Write 24 on the biggest advent window in black pen. Randomly add numbers 1–23 to the rest of the windows.

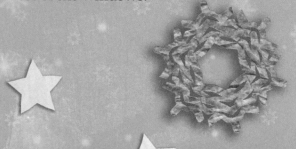

Snow-globe Terrarium

This pretty snow globe makes a nice addition to a Christmas display. Save different-sized jars so you can make a few.

You will need

- Jar with a lid, about 2 pints (1 litre)
- Handful of decorative moss
- Battery-operated fairy lights
- Cotton wool balls
- Fake snow or glitter
- Mini white pompoms
- Bottle-brush Christmas tree small enough to fit in your jar

- Craft glue
- Pencil
- Scrap of corrugated cardboard
- Fishing wire, about 40in (1m)
- Needle
- Ribbon or rickrack
- Adhesive tape
- Scissors

1 Start by putting moss at the bottom of the jar.

2 Add fairy lights to the jar, then add a layer of torn-up cotton wool balls.

3 Sprinkle fake snow or glitter on top and add some mini pompoms.

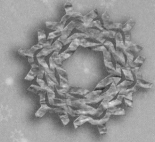

4 Wrap the fairy lights around the bottle-brush tree, leaving enough wire for the battery pack to sit outside the jar. Add glue to the base of the tree and stick into the jar.

5 Draw around the inner rim of the lid onto corrugated cardboard, then cut out. Thread three or four pompoms on to seven pieces of fishing wire about 6in (15cm) long.

6 Then thread the wire through the cardboard circle and tape to secure.

7 Glue the cardboard into the lid and screw back onto the jar.

8 Glue on decorative trim such as rickrack around the lid to finish.

Festive Story Stones

Part of the fun for this activity is getting out and finding a selection of lovely smooth pebbles for your story stones. But if you don't have a beach nearby, you can pick up pebbles from garden and craft stores. We used a sewing machine for the bag, but you could stitch it by hand.

For the Story Stones
You will need

- About 10 pebbles (see step 1)
- Pencil
- Acrylic pens or paint
- Fine permanent pens
- Craft varnish
- Paintbrushes

For the Festive Bag
You will need

- 10 x 17in (25 x 43cm) rectangle of red fabric
- Iron
- Needle and thread
- Scrap paper
- Scraps of green and gray fabrics
- Scraps of fusible interfacing
- Mini pompoms
- Fabric glue
- 20in (50cm) ribbon
- Safety pin
- Sewing pins
- Pinking shears (optional)
- Scissors

How to play

Use your stones to create funny festive stories. Pull a stone from the bag without looking and use the picture as a starting point for your story. Gradually pull out more stones and add the subjects to your tale. It will be different every time.

1 Start by gathering 10 perfect pebbles for your story stones. These should be between 1½ and 2½in (4–6cm) and have a nice smooth surface.

2 Use a pencil to mark out festive pictures on the rocks. You will need a mixture of festive people, places, and objects.

3 Fill in the pencil marks with acrylic pens or paint. Leave to dry.

4 Add smaller details with permanent pen. Follow with a slick of varnish to make them a little more durable.

5 Take the red fabric and fold both the short edges in by ½in (1cm) and press with an iron. Fold over one of the long edges by ½in (1cm). Press. Fold in again by 1in (2.5cm). Sew along the bottom of this fold, to create a channel for the ribbon.

6 Fold the fabric in half widthways, with the folded edges on the outside. Pin and sew around the edge of the bag with a ¼in (5mm) seam allowance, starting from just underneath the sewn channel and continuing all down the side and bottom. Trim the raw edges (pinking shears are good for this if you have them, as they reduce fraying). Then turn the bag the right way out.

7 For the tree appliqué, draw a triangle (about 4in/10cm high) and a square (about 1½in/4cm) on a scrap of paper and cut out. Iron some fusible interfacing onto the back of the green and gray fabrics. Use your templates to cut out the two shapes from the fabrics. Position your tree pieces centrally on the bag and press.

8 Glue mini pompoms onto the tree. Then attach the ribbon to a safety pin and feed it through the channel in the bag.

Stamped Gift Tags and Cards

Kids love to get messy with stamping, and these two techniques are really simple and fun. Turn your prints into Christmas wrapping paper, cards, or gift tags.

For the Potato Stamp Gift Tags
You will need

- Medium-sized potato
- Pencil
- Sharp knife
- Paper towels
- Paint
- Paintbrush
- Card to print on
- Scissors

For the Foam Stamp Christmas Cards
You will need

- Scraps of craft foam
- Pencil
- Scissors
- Scraps of corrugated card
- Craft glue
- Paint
- Paintbrush
- Blank cards

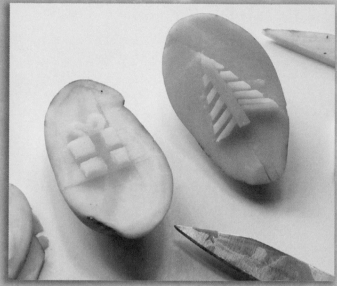

1 For the gift tags, slice the potato in half and mark on a simple design with a sharp pencil onto the flat edge.

2 Ask an adult to use a sharp knife to cut out the stamp. Cut along the outline of the shape about ¼in (5mm) deep, then hold the knife flat and cut in towards the shape, ¼in (5mm) deep, as if you were cutting a flat slice.

3 Pat the potato halves with paper towels to remove any excess water, then either dip the potatoes into a thin layer of paint, or dab it onto the potato with a paintbrush. Line it up carefully and stamp onto your card in rows.

4 Once dry, cut out each stamped section to make your gift tags.

1 For the Christmas cards, draw out your designs onto craft foam. Here we drew circles with various patterns for Christmas ornaments that were roughly 1½in (4cm).

2 Cut out your designs, making sure to cut out any patterns or shapes within them (small sharp scissors are good for this). Cut circles of corrugated card that are a little bigger than the stamps and glue the foam, pencil side down, to the middle.

3 On the other side of the card, mark a T to indicate the top of your stamp, to help you line it up on the card. Then, as with the potato stamps, you can dip the stamps into a thin layer of paint, or add it to the foam with a brush. Press down onto the blank cards with a steady hand. Gently remove the stamp and repeat to fill your card.

Natural Decorations

These three nature crafts are a great excuse to get out on a walk to gather materials, then spend a cozy afternoon making them!

For the Reindeer Wreath
You will need

- Corrugated card (dinner plate size)
- Pencil
- Scissors
- 10–15 pine cones
- Pruning clippers
- Googly eyes (two per pine cone)
- Craft glue
- About 30 red and 15 green pompoms
- Permanent black pen
- Handful of twigs
- 20in (50cm) twine

1 Draw around a dinner plate onto card, then draw around a bowl in the middle to create a ring that is about 8in (20cm) in diameter and 1½in (4cm) wide. Cut this out and make another one the same size.

2 Ask an adult to cut the top third of the pine cones off with pruning clippers so you get a nice flat top.

3 Glue googly eyes and a red pompom nose onto the base of each pine cone (the uncut part) and add a smile with permanent pen.

4 Glue the pine cones onto the cardboard wreath with the smiles facing into the middle of the wreath.

5 Glue the twigs onto the back of the card base around the outside to make antlers. Then glue the second cardboard base onto the back.

6 Stick red and green pompoms in the gaps around the wreath. Add a hanging loop by folding the twine in half and gluing it onto the back of the wreath at the top.

For the Twig Stars You will need

- Thin twigs (5 per star)
- Craft glue
- Pruning clippers
- Mini pompoms
- Wool

1 Ask an adult to cut the twigs to roughly 6in (15cm). Arrange five of them into a star as shown. Glue in place at the ends.

2 Glue pompoms onto the sticks and leave to dry.

3 Cut a piece of wool to 15in (38cm) and tie it onto the top point of the star.

For the Twig Tree
You will need

- Corrugated card
- Pencil
- Scissors
- Handful of twigs
- Paint
- Paintbrush
- Glitter
- Pruning clippers
- Craft glue
- Yellow pompoms
- Twine

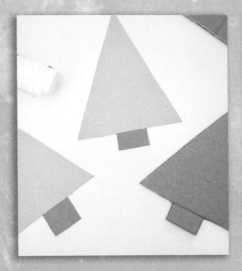

1 Draw and cut out a simple tree shape in corrugated card. These measured 5in (12cm) tall and 4in (10cm) wide with a 1in (2.5cm) trunk.

2 Paint the twigs in various colors and add a sprinkle of glitter. Leave to dry.

3 Ask an adult to measure and cut the twigs using pruning clippers to fit across the tree.

4 Glue onto the card. Glue plain twigs vertically on the trunk and leave to dry.

5 Add a yellow pompom on top for the star.

6 Glue a loop of twine for hanging at the back.

Wooden Spoon Puppets

Put on your very own festive show with these simple spoon puppets.

We've made Santa, Rudolph, and a twinkly angel, but you could make any

Christmas characters you like: a snowman, elf, or penguin perhaps.

You will need

- 3 large wooden spoons
- Brown acrylic paint
- Paintbrush
- PVA glue
- Black, white, red, pink, beige, green, brown, and gold felt scraps
- Scissors
- Strong glue
- 2 sparkly pipe cleaners
- 6 googly eyes
- White, pink, blue, and red pompoms
- Festive sequins
- Permanent marker pen
- Small round bell

1 Paint one of the spoons brown. Leave to dry before adding a coat of PVA glue to all three spoons. Leave to dry. Note that the back of the spoons will be the front from now on!

2 Cut out the felt pieces as indicated on the templates (see page 139).

3 To make Santa, start by gluing the black leg piece around the spoon handle. Line up the bottom of the felt with the end of the spoon. Wrap the coat just under the head, overlap the edges at the front, and glue together. Wrap the black belt around the middle of the coat and glue at the back. Glue the beard on, followed by the hat.

4 For Rudolph, glue the snout onto the front of the brown-painted spoon. Glue the antlers and ears on to the back so that they are poking out over the top. Glue the collar around his neck.

5 Fold over the narrow edge of the angel dress by 1in (2.5cm). Fold again so the two straight edges meet with a ¼in (5mm) overlap. Check the gap at the top is big enough for the spoon handle, then glue.

6 Glue the angel hair on top of the spoon, slide on the dress, with the seam at the back, and glue in place around the neck.

7 Make angel wings by bending both ends of a sparkly pipe cleaner into the middle and twisting to hold. Glue onto some gold felt, leave to dry, then trim away the excess.

8 Twist a pipe cleaner into a circle about 1½in (4cm) wide. Twist the ends together and glue to the back of the angel's head. Bend the circle down over the head. Glue the angel wings onto the back of the spoon.

9 Add googly eyes to each puppet. Decorate Santa's hat with white pompoms and add a pink one for his nose. Add a gold sequin as a buckle and draw on a smile. Add blue pompoms around the angel's collar and a large pink one for a bun, then embellish her dress with festive sequins. Add a red pompom to Rudolph for his nose and a little bell to his collar.

Cuddly Creature Hand Warmers

These snuggly creatures are the perfect pocket companion to keep your hands warm on a chilly day. We've sewn them together using a machine but you could hand sew them. They are filled with rice, which holds its heat really well when warmed in a microwave. If you want, you could even add some dried lavender to create a lovely scent when heated.

You will need

- 2 sheets of felt, 9 x 12in (23 x 30cm), one white and one gray
- Scrap of black felt
- Needle and black, white, and gray sewing thread
- 4 black buttons
- Funnel or teaspoon
- About a cup of rice
- Sewing pins
- Scissors

How to...

Blanket stitch

Blanket stitch looks like a row of open boxes. Pull your needle up on the baseline. Push it back down where the top of the adjoining box shape will go (A), and out at the base of that box (B). Make sure the thread is under the needle before you pull it through. Repeat.

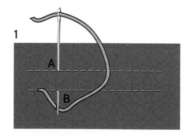
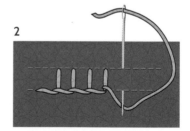

Slip stitch

To close your item after you have stuffed it, fold your fabric at each side of the gap to match the seams so far. Push your needle through from inside the fold on one side so that the knot is hidden. Push your needle into the opposite fold directly across from where the thread came out. Push it back out a little way along the fold. Then push it into the fold on the other side directly across. Repeat until you have closed the gap.

1 Cut out the felt pieces as indicated on the templates (see page 138). For the bear, cut two heads and four ears from white, two inner ears and one snout from gray, and one nose from black. For the penguin, cut two heads from gray, one face from white, and one beak from black.

2 For the polar bear, use gray thread to hand or machine sew the inner ears onto the outer ears using blanket stitch (see page 40). Make sure the flat edges are lined up along the bottom. Then pin and sew the gray snout onto a head piece, 1in (2.5cm) from the bottom.

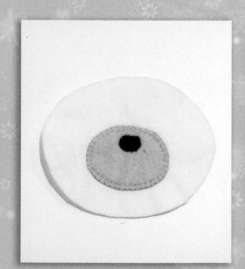

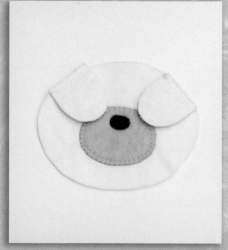

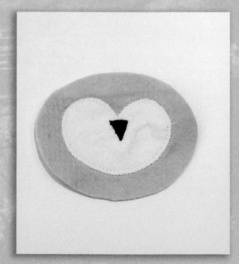

3 Use black thread to sew the nose onto the snout, ¼in (5mm) from the top.

4 Line up the ears on top of the head, facing in, with the raw edges of the ears and head lined up. Pin and sew just in from the edge of the felt.

5 For the penguin, pin the face onto the middle of one of the head pieces and sew in place. Then sew the beak on in the middle of the face.

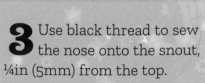

6 Mark and hand sew buttons for eyes on both hand warmers.

7 Place the head pieces with faces on top of the other head pieces, face down. Sew with a ¼in (5mm) seam allowance, leaving a ½in (1cm) gap at the bottom.

8 Trim the excess felt, then make snips almost to the seam, all the way around. This will prevent puckering. Turn the hand warmers the right way out.

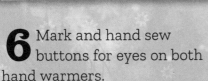

9 Use a funnel or teaspoon to fill the hand warmers with rice. Don't over fill them or it will be tricky to stitch up the opening.

10 Stitch the opening closed with slip stitch (see page 40). Then all you need to do is pop the hand warmers in the microwave for 20 seconds to heat the rice, and pop them in your pockets.

Quick Christmas Tree Decorations

These quick tree decorations are a fun activity to do while you're waiting for Santa to arrive. The pretty suncatchers look great on the Christmas tree with twinkly lights shining behind them.

For the Cardboard Tree Suncatcher
You will need

- Corrugated card
- Pencil
- Scissors
- Green paint and paintbrush
- Clear sticky-backed plastic (contact paper)
- Tissue paper
- Sequins
- Glitter
- Glue stick
- Handful of sequins
- Twine

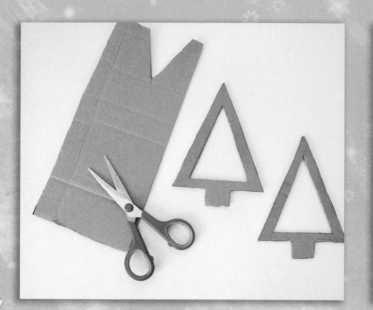

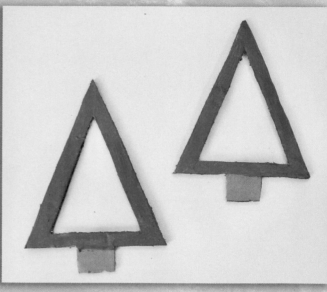

1 Draw a simple tree shape on corrugated card and cut out. Cut out the middle triangle to create a tree-shaped frame. For each decoration cut out two trees.

2 Paint each frame green, leaving the trunk brown, and leave to dry.

3 Cut out two triangles of sticky-backed plastic the same size as the frame (draw around the frame as a guide). Totally cover one piece with small pieces of tissue paper, sequins, and a sprinkling of glitter.

4 Stick the other triangle of sticky-backed plastic on top and trim.

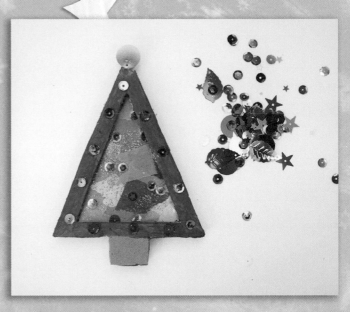

5 Glue the sticky-backed plastic onto the back of one of the cardboard trees and glue the other tree on the back.

6 Glue sequins on the front and add a larger sequin on top of the tree for the star.

7 Cut a hanging loop from twine, fold in half, and glue onto the back of the tree.

For the Spin Art Ornaments You will need

- Sheet of corrugated card
- Pencil
- Jar lid about 3in (8cm) in diameter
- Sheet of metallic card
- Adhesive putty

- Salad spinner
- Washable paint
- Glitter
- Scrap of colored card
- Glue stick
- Metallic ribbon (10in/25cm for each ornament)

Tip

Art with a salad spinner is one that kids will particularly enjoy. But if you don't have one you could always use the paint-splattered effect used on the crackers on page 108.

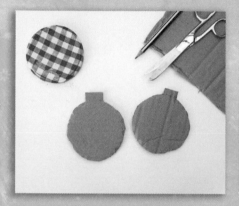

1 Draw ornament shapes on corrugated card by using a lid as a template (this one measured 3in/8cm) and adding a small rectangle for the top. Cut your ornaments out.

2 Draw around the lid again on metallic card and cut out two circles per ornament. Use adhesive putty to stick one inside the base of the salad spinner, shiny side up.

3 Add small drops of paint into the middle of the card on the shiny side. The paint needs to be a little runny so if you are using very thick paint water it down a little.

4 Put the lid on and get spinning. Once you've spun you can open the lid, add more paint and spin again! Sprinkle glitter onto the ornament and leave to dry.

5 Cut a piece of scrap colored card into a rectangle and glue onto the top of the corrugated card ornament. Then glue one of the pieces of painted metallic card on top.

6 Cut a 10in (25cm) piece of ribbon, fold in half, and glue onto the back of the ornament. Glue a second rectangle of colored card onto the back and glue the other piece of painted metallic card on top.

For the Tissue Paper Wreath
You will need

- Corrugated card
- Pencil
- 2 jar lids about 3in (8cm) and 2in (5cm) in diameter

- Scissors
- Glue stick
- Colorful tissue paper
- Sequins
- Length of twine, about 6in (15cm)

1 Draw around a lid onto corrugated card. Ours measured 3in (8cm) in diameter. Draw around a smaller lid (ours measured 2in/5cm) inside the circle and cut out to create a ring.

2 Screw up small squares of tissue paper and glue onto the cardboard wreath to cover.

4 Cut a length of twine, fold in half, and glue onto the back.

3 Glue sequins around the wreath.

49

Christmas Sweaters

You've got the house decorated and the presents ready, but you've got nothing to wear! These easy no-sew upcycled Christmas outfits will have you looking festive in a flash.

You will need

- Old sweater
- Pencil
- Large plastic bag
- Fabric glue
- Large piece of paper

For the Rudolph Sweater

- 40in (100cm) sequin trim
- 2 black buttons
- Red pompom

For the Tree Sweater

- Pompoms in assorted colors, including brown

1 For the Rudolph sweater use the antler template (see page 141) to draw the pattern on the sweater. The top tip of the antler should be roughly in line with the neck of the sweater. Draw around it with pencil then flip the template over and draw the other antler on the other side of the sweater.

2 Slide a plastic bag inside the sweater to stop glue going onto the back. Then add a line of glue to the pencil marks and glue on the sequin trim around both antlers. Leave to dry.

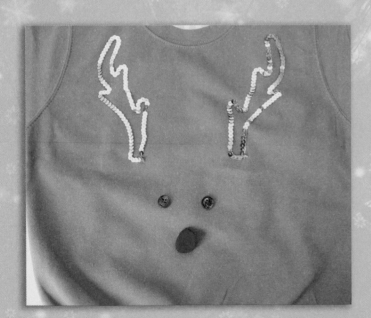

3 Position the button eyes and pompom nose on the sweater and glue in place.

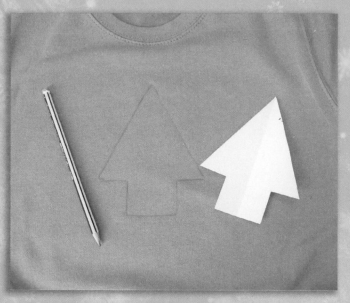

4 For the tree sweater, draw yourself a simple tree template on paper and cut it out (our triangle shape was 4in/10cm tall and wide, and the square trunk was about 1½in/4cm). Use this template to mark the pattern in pencil onto the sweater.

5 Slide a plastic bag inside the sweater. Use fabric glue to attach brown pompoms for the tree trunk.

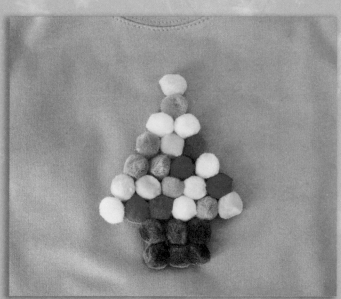

6 Glue on a colorful assortment of pompoms for the tree and a yellow pompom as the star on top. Leave to dry.

Nutcracker Skittles

Make yourself a set of these adorable festive skittles based on the characters in *The Nutcracker*. Use the templates provided (see page 140) or make up your own if you prefer. Note that you may have to adjust the sizes for the templates depending on the size of your tubes.

You will need

- 5 cardboard tubes
- Scraps of card
- Pencil
- Scissors
- Craft glue
- About ¹⁄₂ cup rice/pulses
- Gray and skin-color paints
- Paintbrushes
- Card in the following colors: white, black, yellow, pale blue, dark blue, red, green, gray, and pink
- Double-sided tape
- Felt tip pens
- 1 black and 2 yellow pompoms
- 1 sequin

1 Place a cardboard tube onto a scrap of card and draw around the end of it to create a circle. Draw around this circle with a ¼in (5mm) border. Cut out and use as a template to create 10 more circles.

2 Cut tabs into each circle, ¼in (5mm) apart and deep, then bend the tabs up. Glue to one end of each tube.

3 Pour two tablespoons of rice into each tube, then seal them up with the remaining circles, as before.

4 Paint the tubes. Paint one gray and the rest in different skin shades. Leave to dry.

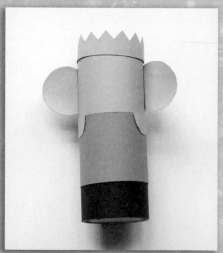

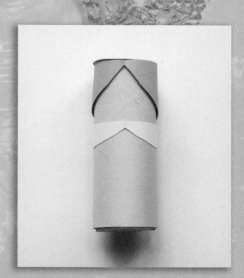

5 Using the templates (see page 140) cut out the hair and clothes pieces from colored card as indicated.

6 Use the gray tube for the Mouse King. Fold the gray ears along the tab and use tape or glue to attach. Add the black base then wrap the green top above it so it overlaps. Attach the epaulets either side then wrap the gold crown at the top.

7 For Clara, tape the light blue dress around one of the remaining tubes, lining it up with the bottom. Add the white rounded collar to the top of the dress. Attach the yellow head piece and hair to the top of the tube.

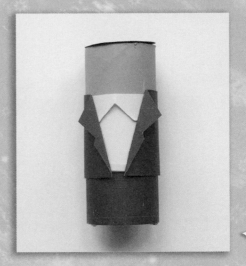

8 For the Nutcracker, glue a black circle to the top then wrap the black hat piece underneath it, and glue or tape in place. Attach the black base with a red jacket over the top. Add a yellow belt over the jacket.

9 For the Sugar Plum Fairy, cut slits into the pink dress piece, ⅛in (3mm) apart and 1½in (4cm) deep. Bend and curl the slits up to look like a tutu, then glue around the tube. Attach the black hair and head pieces to the top.

10 For the Prince, tape the blue base and a white top to the tube. Attach the white pointed collar and yellow belt on top. Fold the blue jacket piece as shown and tape in place over the collar. Add a black circle to the top.

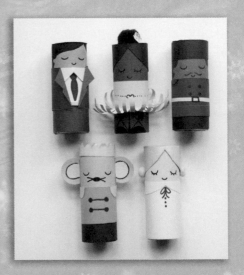

11 Add features, such as faces, hair, and decorative bows or buttons, to the skittles using felt tip pens.

12 Finally, add a pompom and sequin to the top of the fairy and two for buns on the sides of Clara's head.

13 To play, line up the skittles with two in the front and three in the back. Roll a ball towards them and see how many you can knock down. If you have hoops you could also use these for a simple ring toss game.

Santa's Elf

Would you like to make your own unique, cheeky elf? This one comes complete with little belled booties and a hat and a bag to store his goodies in. This is a lovely project that will be loved for many years. Start well ahead of December as this is one of the more complicated projects and may take some time!

You will need

- Pale beige thick cotton (about 10in/25cm square)
- Brown felt (about 6in/15cm square)
- Needle and thread in various shades to match the fabrics
- Pencil
- Black, red, and green embroidery thread and embroidery needle
- Scraps of pink and white felt
- A few handfuls of toy stuffing
- Scissors
- 3 matching Christmas print cottons in cream, gray, and red (about 12in/30cm square of each)

- ¼ cup rice
- Funnel
- Green cotton (about 6in/15cm square)
- Scrap of thin iron-on interfacing
- 1 medium and 2 small bells
- 8in (20cm) red bias binding, about ³⁄₄in (1.5cm) wide
- 1 tiny decorative button
- Sewing pins

Please note this project uses a ¹⁄₄in (5mm) seam allowance unless stated.

How to...
Back stitch

Using the illustration as a guide, bring the needle up through the back of the fabric at A, about ¹⁄₈in (3mm) along the line you want to stitch. Push the needle back down at B. Bring the needle up again at C, and then down again at A. Work along like this to create a neat continuous line.

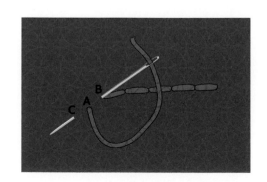

1 Use the templates (see pages 137–138) to cut out all the pattern pieces as indicated. Pin the front and back hair pieces onto the head pieces and sew in place right along the bottom edge of the hair.

2 Mark in pencil some eyes and a little mouth in the middle of the face and back stitch with embroidery thread in black and red. Cut some small circles from pink felt for rosy cheeks and sew these in place next to the smile.

3 Pin the ears onto the side of the face, facing in with the edges lined up. Sew just along the edge to secure. Place the head pieces right sides together and sew. Snip round the curves in the seam allowance and turn out carefully, then stuff.

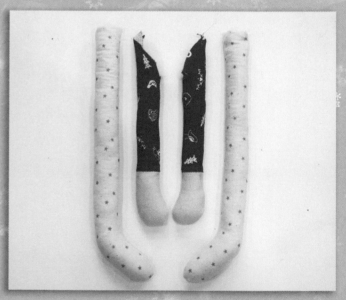

4 To make the arms and legs, pin and sew the hand pieces onto the arm pieces, facing in, with the flat edges lined up. Open out and press the seams flat. Pin and sew the arm pieces right sides together, then repeat for the leg pieces. Turn out and stuff all the limbs.

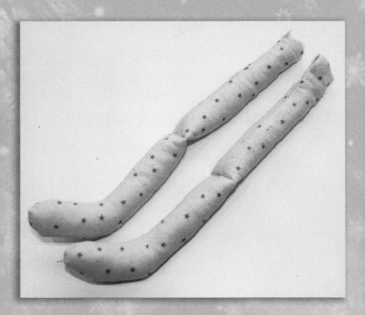

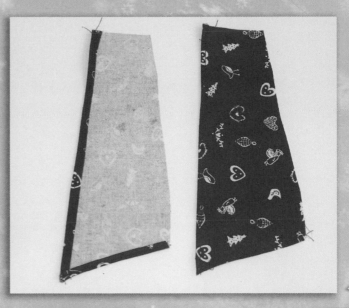

5 Add a little knee hinge to the legs by sewing across the middle of each leg.

6 Fold the long edges of the coat over twice by a fraction of an inch (a few millimeters). Pin and sew to create a neat edge. Repeat for the bottom edge.

7 Place the gray body piece face up in front of you, then lay the coat pieces on top facing up, with the top raw outside edges lined up. Pin and sew along the side edges to hold in place.

8 Pin the arms onto the right sides of the coat, facing inwards with the raw edges lined up. Sew along the edges to secure.

9 Then pin the red body piece on top, right sides together and sew together along the sides. Turn right sides out.

10 Fold the top edges of the body in to hide the raw edges and insert the head. Hand stitch in place. Pin the collar piece on and sew on using decorative embroidery thread. We added a little flower using back stitch (see page 58).

11 Pin the legs onto the bottom of the front body piece, right sides together. The legs should be pointing upwards with the edges lined up. Sew in place and stuff the body.

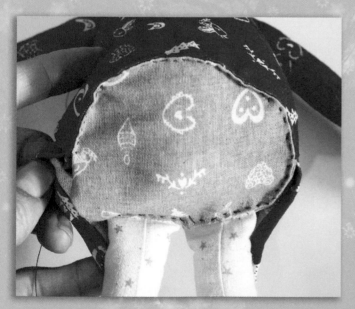

12 Cut tabs into the base piece, about 1¼in (3cm) apart and ½in (1cm) long. Fold the tabs up and pin them inside the body, with the right side of the fabric at the bottom. Hand sew in place, leaving 1½in (4cm) open. Using a funnel, pour in the rice through this hole, then sew the gap to seal.

13 For the hat, pin and sew the hat trim right sides together to the base of the hat (lined up with the straight section of the hat). Fold the raw edge under, pin and sew, leaving a trim of ¼in (5mm). Use a contrasting thread and sew along the middle of the trim.

14 Sew the pieces together then turn out. Cut out two tiny leaves in green fabric. Stitch down the middle in green and sew to the hat with red embroidery thread. Sew the bigger bell to the top.

15 To make the boots, take some red bias binding and pin it over the top of the green boot pieces. Sew to hide the raw edges. You can do all the boot pieces in one lot to save time!

16 Pin and sew the pairs of boot pieces right sides together. Turn right sides out, then sew a small bell onto the end of each. Slide the boots onto his feet.

17 For the bag, cut another strip measuring 8 x 2½in (20 x 6cm). Fold all the edges in by ¼in (5mm) and sew. Fold one end in by 1½in (4cm) and sew all the way around to make the top of the bag. Fold the other end in by 2in (5cm) and sew the sides, leaving the inside open.

18 For the bag strap, cut a rectangle of fabric measuring 12 x 1in (30 x 2.5cm). Press the sides in by ¼in (5mm), then fold in half and pin to hide the edges. Sew to secure. Use a decorative stitch if you like. Hand stitch the ends to the back and add a little decorative button to the front.

Paper Lanterns

These tissue paper lanterns are simple to make but take a bit of time and patience to stick together. Put a festive movie on and get cutting and sticking!

You will need

- Thin card
- Pencil
- Scissors
- Plenty of tissue paper in any color you like
- Large piece of paper
- Colored pens in red and blue, or other strong colors
- Ruler
- Adhesive tape
- Glue stick
- Sewing thread and needle
- Paper clips (optional)

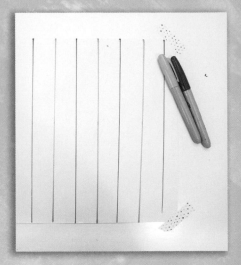

1 Draw a circle the size you want your lanterns to be onto a piece of card. This one measures 6in (15cm) in diameter. Cut out then cut in half.

2 Cut the tissue paper into pieces bigger than the semicircle. These lanterns had 50 sheets of tissue paper each. For fuller looking lanterns add more sheets of tissue paper.

3 Lay a large piece of paper sideways and draw vertical lines 1¼in (3cm) apart using red and blue pens, alternating the colors as you go across the page. Tape the paper down to your work surface.

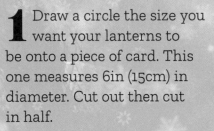

4 Lay the first piece of tissue paper on top of the lined piece of paper. Looking through the tissue paper to the colored lines underneath, use a glue stick to draw a thin line of glue down all of the red lines. Place another piece of tissue paper on top and press down.

5 Add a line of glue down all the blue lines and attach a piece of tissue paper on top. Add more layers of tissue paper on top remembering to alternate the colored lines you glue on each layer. You'll still see the colored lines on the paper above and below your tissue paper. Keep layering until you have about 50 sheets of paper.

6 Lay the semicircle template on top of the tissue paper, lining up one of the long edges of the tissue paper with the flat edge of the semicircle. Draw around it and cut the tissue paper out into a semicircle shape. If you have excess glued tissue paper, you can use it to make smaller lanterns.

7 Trim a little off the rounded edge of each of the semicircle cards to make it a little smaller. Cut the semicircles of card into arches about 1in (2.5cm) wide. Glue onto either side of the tissue paper stack.

8 Push a threaded needle through both corners of the tissue paper. Tie the ends together but keep the thread loose and long.

9 Open up the lantern and glue or paper clip the cardboard arches together. Using paper clips will allow you to fold up the lantern to be used again.

10 Trim the loose thread at one end of the lantern and use the thread at the top to hang it. Make lots more in different colors.

Seasonal String Art

The fun thing about this project is that you could make any shape you like as long as it can be recognized as a silhouette. We have made a tree, but you could make other things, such as a message or a star.

You will need

- 12in (30cm) square of ½in (1cm) thick plywood
- White paint and paintbrushes
- Sandpaper (optional)
- Masking or painter's tape
- 80 copper nails (¾in/2cm long)
- Hammer
- Green, brown, and yellow sewing thread
- Craft glue
- Colorful mini pompoms or sequins
- Scissors
- Picture hanger (optional)

Tip
You can find plywood cut to size online or at wood stores. Make sure the wood is at least ½in (1cm) thick to allow for the nails.

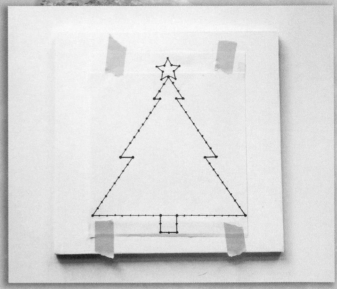

1 Paint the square of plywood all over with two coats of white paint. If the surface feels rough after the first coat, sand it down before adding the second coat. Leave to dry.

2 Photocopy the template (see page 141) and line it up centrally on the plywood. Tape in place.

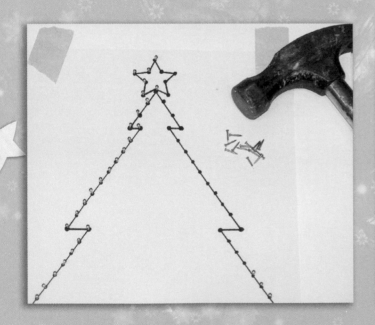

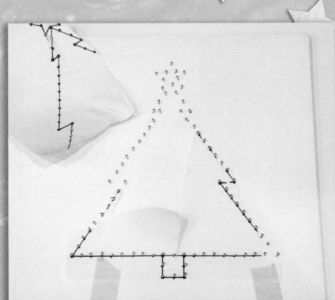

3 Working around the template, ask an adult to use a hammer to hit the nails into the plywood where indicated by dots on the template. Hammer them in until roughly ½in (1cm) of the nail is still visible.

4 Carefully tear the paper to remove the template from the wood.

5 Tie some green thread, still on the reel, to the top of the tree. Holding the thread taut, bring the thread to the first nail on the left and wrap around it twice. Work your way down the tree in this way, zigzagging left to right and back again. When you get to the bottom, work back up using the opposite nails, then tie to secure.

6 Tie yellow thread onto a nail for the star, then work round the different points to make a pattern. Tie brown thread to a nail for the tree base then wrap it round the other nails to make a pattern. Tie to secure, then snip away the loose threads and add a small dot of glue to the knot to prevent it from coming loose.

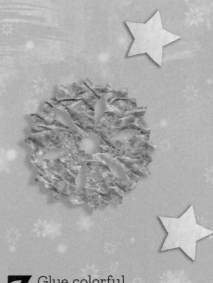

7 Glue colorful pompoms or sequins to the tree for ornaments. If you like you can add a picture hanger to the back of your art, or simply prop it up on a shelf.

Copper Star Light

These pretty copper lights are a lovely way to festive-up a window or wall. Using battery-operated lights gives you the freedom to hang them anywhere you like. You could use plug-in ones if you prefer, but just remember to leave enough cable to reach the socket.

You will need

- 5 lengths of thin copper tube (these ones measured 1³⁄₄ x 12in/4.5 x 30cm)
- 70in (180cm) copper (or other) wire, 12 gauge (2mm)
- Pliers
- Wire cutters
- Copper wire fairy lights (at least 160in/4m long)
- Metal file
- Fishing wire
- Scissors

Tip

Thin copper tubing can be bought easily online, but don't fret if you can't get hold of it because this project is just as lovely with 12-gauge copper wire. The end result will just be a little more bendable.

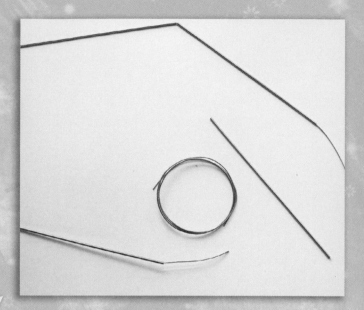

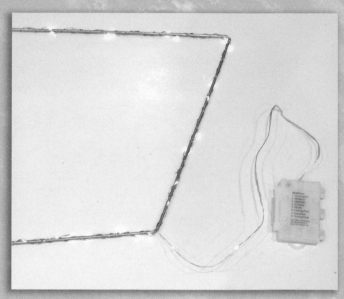

1 Carefully feed the five copper tube pieces onto the wire, like beads. Bend any kinks in the wire with pliers to make getting the tubes on easier. Once they are all on the wire, adjust so that there is 4in (10cm) excess at each end.

2 Twist the copper fairy lights all the way along the copper pipes. It can help to have the lights on for this, so you can see how they are spaced. When you reach the end of the piping, go back the other way. Make sure to finish on a gap in the pipes. Leave enough excess wire for the battery pack to sit below the light. Test the light in its intended location to be sure.

3 Bend the pipe into a star. Start with the join that has the end of the wire, and bend so that this section creates a point. Fold in the rest of the joins, overlapping, to create a five-point star as shown in the picture. Once you are happy with the shape, use the pliers to twist the ends of the wire tightly together. Ask an adult to help.

4 Trim off the excess wire and file to smooth the rough edges.

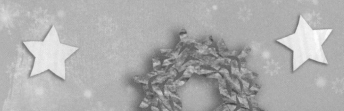

5 Add a length of fishing wire around one of the points (with the wire battery pack at the bottom) and hang the star on a hook.

Star ideas

Twig star lights: Glue twigs into a star shape (see page 32) then wrap fairy lights around it.

Yarn-wrapped stars: Cut a star shape from cardboard and wrap different-colored yarn around it. Secure the yarn at the back with tape.

Paper straw stars: If you have festive paper straws then you can glue them together in a star shape, tie thread around the top, and hang them on the Christmas tree.

Elf and Fairy Peg Dolls

These little friends make lovely festive decorations and you can peg them directly onto your tree. If you like you could add a small length of ribbon to allow you to hang them up. Or make lots of different characters and have an elf and fairy hunt.

You will need

- 2 wooden dolly pegs
- Green, gray, and white acrylic paint and paintbrush
- PVA glue
- Scraps of red and silver fabric
- Scrap of iron-on interfacing and an iron (optional)
- Scraps of yellow and green felt
- Craft glue
- Pompom
- 12 x 2½in (30cm x 6cm) sparkly tulle
- Needle and white thread
- Oddment of pink wool
- Scrap of silver card
- Permanent marker pens
- Scissors

How to...

Running stitch

Knot the end of the thread and push the needle through from the back of the fabric. Insert the needle back in to the left of where the thread came through. The stitch can be as long as you like. Repeat all along the line you want to stitch, keeping the stitches even.

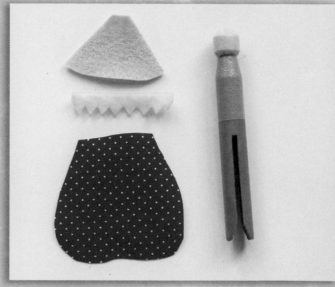

1 Paint one of the pegs gray and green (to look like legs and a top) and the other one white. Leave the heads unpainted. Once dry, add a coat of PVA glue all over.

2 Using the templates (see page 139) cut out the cape from red fabric for the elf. You can iron interfacing to the reverse to add a bit of stiffness and prevent fraying. From felt, cut a yellow collar and green hat.

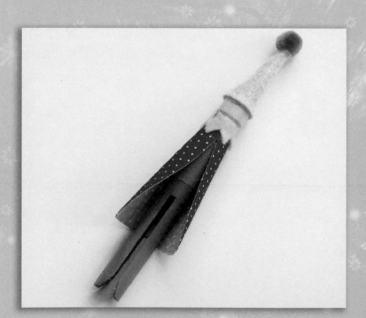

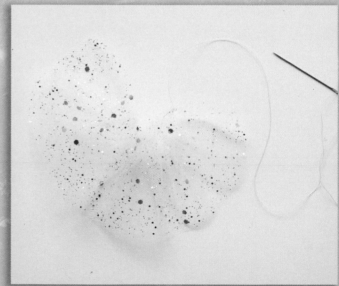

3 Glue the cape around the body of the elf, making sure the gap for the legs is at the front. Glue the yellow collar around the neck. Wrap the hat around the head and glue the ends together. (You can pop another peg on the hat to hold it in place while it sets if you need to). Add a pompom on top of the hat to finish.

4 For the fairy, take the length of tulle and stitch one of the corners to secure. Then stitch all along one of the long edges, about ¼in (5mm) from the edge, using nice wide running stitches (see page 76). Once you get to the end, gently pull the thread to gather the fabric until it is just wide enough to go around the peg. Hand stitch a knot in the corner to secure.

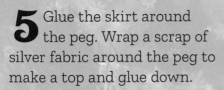

5 Glue the skirt around the peg. Wrap a scrap of silver fabric around the peg to make a top and glue down.

6 Cut 7–10 pieces of pink wool measuring about 4in (10cm). Add some glue to the top of the fairy's head (avoiding the face) and add the strands to the head. Trim to an even length.

7 Fold the silver card in half. Draw one side of a set of wings, starting at the fold. Unfold and use as a template to cut out another set. Glue wrong sides together, then stick to the fairy's back.

8 To finish, use permanent pens to add face, shoe, and jewelry details to the elf and fairy.

9 If you like you can make more fairies and elves with different fabrics and styles.

Christmas Cake Cushion

Super soft and cheery, this cushion (based on British Christmas puddings) adds a cozy festive feel to your living room. We made it 12in (30cm) in diameter but you can make it any size you like.

You will need

- ½yd (50cm) brown velvety material
- ½yd (50cm) white velvety material
- Pencil
- Scissors
- Sewing pins
- White sewing thread and needle
- White embroidery thread and needle
- 5oz (150g) toy stuffing
- Ball of red wool

Tip

It's best to use a sewing machine for this project. It can be made by hand, just make sure you stick to thinner fabrics.

1 Draw two large circles onto brown fabric (these measure 12in/30cm in diameter) and cut them out. For the white topping of the cushion draw around half the brown circle and draw wiggly lines along the bottom. Use this as a template to draw another one for the back.

2 Pin the white fabric onto the brown pieces, lining up the outer curve. Use a sewing machine to sew together along the wiggly line with a blanket or zigzag stitch. If your machine can't do this then you can do it by hand (see page 40). Repeat for the other side.

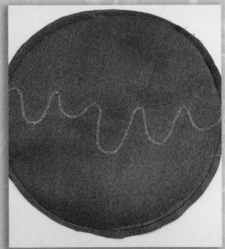

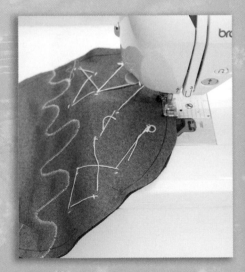

3 With white embroidery thread, hand stitch a few simple crosses onto the brown part of one of the sides of the cushion.

4 Pin the two cushion pieces right sides together lining up the white pieces and the top edges.

5 Sew around the cushion with a ½in (1cm) seam allowance leaving about 6in (15cm) unsewn so the cushion can be turned out.

6 Trim any excess fabric around the edges and add little snips in the seam allowance to prevent puckering.

7 Turn the cushion the right way out and stuff with toy stuffing so it's nice and plump.

8 Hand sew the opening closed using a slip stitch (see page 40).

9 Make a pompom by wrapping red wool around your hand about 150 times. Tie a knot tightly around the middle of the bundle and snip through the loops. Neaten up the pompom by snipping it into shape. Hand sew the pompom on top to finish.

Wrapping Paper Photo Frames

These personalized photo-frame ornaments are a great keepsake to hang on the tree each year. They use scraps of wrapping paper and cardboard so are a great way to use up materials that would otherwise go to waste.

You will need

- Corrugated card
- Pencil
- Scissors
- Photos
- Craft glue

- Scraps of wrapping paper
- Wooden skewer
- Glue stick
- Sparkly pipe cleaners

1 Choose what shape you would like your ornament to be. You can use the star or snowflake templates (see pages 138 and 141) or design your own. Just make sure you stick to shapes with straight edges. Draw your shape onto corrugated card and cut it out, making sure it is slightly bigger than your photograph.

2 Trim your photo so that it fits in the middle of your card base with roughly ½in (1cm) around the edge. Glue into place.

3 To make your wrapping paper beads, cut your wrapping paper into evenly sized scraps. These ones measured 5½ x 5½in (14 x 14cm). Begin rolling your scrap a couple of times around a wooden skewer then add a line of glue to prevent it from unravelling. Continue rolling tightly and add another line of glue at the end to seal. Take the bead off the skewer and leave to dry. You will need around 8–12 beads for each ornament.

4 Trim the beads to fit around the outer edges of the card shapes and glue in place. Cut the ends of each bead at an angle if necessary so they fit together nicely.

5 Repeat this so you have two or three rows of beads.

6 Glue sparkly pipe cleaners around the inner rim of the frame. You can make a bow shape from pipe cleaners for the square frame to resemble a present. Embellish further if you like.

7 Fold a pipe cleaner in half and glue onto the back of your ornament to make a hanging loop.

Festive Garland

This festive garland looks great on a mantelpiece or across a wall. You could also put it on your tree or across a window. The possibilities are endless!

You will need

- Felt in an assortment of colors (including dark green)
- Scissors
- Pencil
- Corrugated card
- Oddments of yarn in an assortment of colors
- Ball of twine
- Large-eyed needle
- About 20 bells
- Craft glue

1 Use the templates (see page 140) to cut out the fairy light bulbs in felt from an assortment of colors and the bases from dark green. This garland had 25 lights, but you can cut as many as you like.

2 Glue each bulb onto corrugated card with the green felt overlapping the bottom of the bulb shape. Cut out the cardboard bulbs.

3 Make pompoms in different sizes. For this garland you will need 30–40 pompoms. For the large pompoms, wrap the yarn around a small book 200 times. For medium ones, wrap yarn around your hand 150 times. For small ones wrap it around three fingers 100 times. Slide the bundles off your hand/book.

4 Tie a knot tightly around the middle of each bundle and snip through the loops.

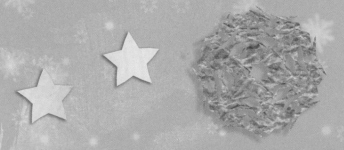

5 Neaten up the pompoms by trimming them into shape.

6 Cut a length of twine (ours measured 160in/4m), then begin threading on your pompoms and bells and sliding them along the twine.

7 Make space on the garland, then arrange and glue the felt fairy lights onto the twine.

Reindeer Antlers

These reindeer antlers are easy to craft and make a great photo prop for a Christmas party, or you could make a batch of them for everyone. Go for a headband that is wide so you can attach the antlers easily.

You will need

- 1 sheet red felt, 9 x 12in (23 x 30cm)
- 2 sheets of brown felt, 9 x 12in (23 x 30cm)
- Scissors
- Wide plastic headband
- Craft glue
- 4 pipe cleaners
- Mini pompoms

1 Use the templates (see page 141) to cut the pieces from felt. Cut four brown antlers from the large template and two red from the smaller template. Then cut approximately 20 brown strips 1in (2.5cm) wide that are long enough to wrap around your headband.

2 Cover the headband in strips of brown felt, gluing each strip next to each other so there are no gaps. Glue so they cover the inside of the headband, trimming the strips to fit the headband neatly.

3 Bend the ends of two pipe cleaners together, to make one long pipe cleaner. Then lay one of the brown felt antler pieces on your work surface and use it as a guide to bend the pipe cleaner into the shape. The pipe cleaners will be glued down the middle of the antlers so make sure there's room. Repeat to make another one.

4 Glue the pipe cleaners down the middle of two of the brown pieces of felt. Then, glue the red felt on top of the other brown pieces of felt. Glue the antlers together with the pipe cleaners in the middle. Leave the bottom 1in (2.5cm) of the antlers unstuck with the pipe cleaners sticking out of the bottom.

5 Twist the pipe cleaners onto the headband and glue the excess felt down onto the inside of the headband. You might need to add a little extra glue to the sides of the antlers just above the headband. Hold the sides together until the glue sets.

6 Cut two strips as wide as the headband out of brown felt. Glue them on top of the ends of the pipe cleaners.

7 Glue mini pompoms along the top of the headband to finish.

String Snowmen

When you haven't any snow but want to build a snowman you can make them from a few simple materials. Make a group of them in different sizes for your own snowman family.

You will need

- 2 balloons
- PVA glue
- Ball of white string
- Sewing pin
- Craft glue
- Scissors
- 1 sheet of black felt, 9 x 12in (23 x 30cm)
- 3 or 4 black buttons
- 1 sheet of orange card, 9 x 12in (23 x 30cm)
- 1 sheet of red felt, 9 x 12in (23 x 30cm)

- Sewing needle and red thread
- A few handfuls of mini pompoms
- 2 twigs
- Pipe cleaner
- Embroidery thread and needle
- A small amount of toy stuffing

1 Blow up the balloons. Inflate one to full size, the other half that for the head.

2 Mix a small amount of water into PVA glue. Dip your string into this paste and wrap it around the balloon. The balloons should be well covered with only small gaps. Repeat for the other balloon and leave overnight to dry.

3 Pop each balloon with a pin and gently remove them, leaving a string mesh structure.

4 Use craft glue to attach the head to the body.

5 Cut two small circles out of black felt for eyes and glue them onto the head. Add buttons for the smile. To make the nose, roll a cone shape out of orange card. You can use the template for the Party Hats (see page 141) for reference. Glue onto the snowman's face.

6 Cut two or three larger circles out of black felt and glue down the middle of the snowman's body for buttons.

7 To make the scarf, cut two strips from the length of the red felt. Stitch them together to make a long strip. Decorate by gluing on pompoms, then cut into each end to make a fringe.

8 Tie the scarf around the snowman's neck and glue twigs onto the sides of the body for the arms.

9 To make earmuffs, cut four circles from red felt (the size will depend on how big your snowman's head is). Glue each end of a pipe cleaner into the middle of two of the felt circles.

11 Bend the pipe cleaner into shape around the snowman's head.

10 Glue mini pompoms on to the other two circles. Pin the circles together with the pipe cleaner sandwiched in the middle then hand sew around the edge using blanket stitch (see page 40). Use a little toy stuffing to make them nice and plump.

Penguin Party Poppers

Create an indoor snowball fight with these little cardboard cannons filled with mini pompoms. You can create any design you like on the front. We went for cute penguins but you could make Santas, snowmen, reindeer, or even make sparkly versions for a New Year's Eve party.

You will need

- 4 cardboard tubes
- Black paint and paintbrush
- 4 balloons
- Scissors
- Duct tape
- 1 sheet black card, 9 x 12in (23 x 30cm)
- 1 sheet white card, 9 x 12in (23 x 30cm)
- Scraps of orange, yellow, green, red, and blue card
- Glue stick
- 8 googly eyes
- Mini white pompoms

1 Begin by painting the cardboard tubes black and leave to dry.

2 Tie a knot in the neck of a balloon and cut off about ½in (1cm) from the other end.

3 Stretch the balloon over the end the tube and add a strip of duct tape around the end of the tube to keep the balloon in place.

4 Use the templates (see page 140) to cut out the penguin shapes from card and glue together. Glue a pair of googly eyes onto each penguin.

5 Glue the penguins onto the front of the cardboard tube, lining up the top of the penguin's head with the top of the tube.

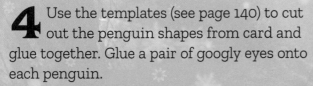

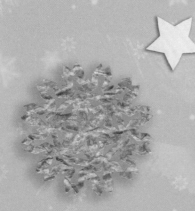

6 To have a snowball fight, load your party popper with mini pompoms, pull back the balloon, aim, and fire. Make sure you don't aim at people's faces.

Party Hats

These party hats made with fringed tissue paper are easy to make and a great activity for kids and adults to make together.

You will need

- 1 sheet of colored card per hat, 9 x 12in (23 x 30cm)
- Scissors
- Glue stick
- Green, red, white, and brown tissue paper
- A handful of small and large multicolored pompoms
- Thin elastic (18in/46cm per hat)
- Needle
- Red and white pipe cleaners
- Green leaf-shaped sequins

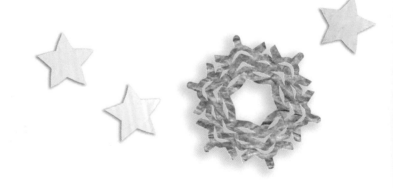

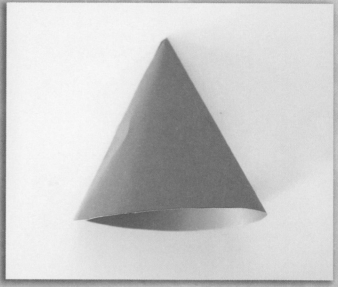

1 To make the Christmas tree hat, use the template (see page 141) to cut out a hat shape from green card. Fold along the dotted line.

2 Add a line of glue along the fold, bend into a cone shape, and press the ends together. Set aside to dry.

3 For the tissue paper fringing, cut strips of green tissue paper 1½in (4cm) wide and cut fringing approximately ¼in (5mm) wide, stopping ½in (1cm) from the top of the tissue paper. Glue the strips on, starting at the bottom of the hat and working up to the top.

4 Make sure there is some overlap between each layer to conceal the top of each strip.

5 Glue pompoms onto the hat as ornaments with a yellow one at the top for a star.

6 Cut 18in (46cm) of thin elastic. Make a hole with a needle ½in (1cm) from the bottom of the hat on either side. Thread elastic through one of the holes and secure with a knot on the inside of the hat. Thread elastic in the hole on the other side, check the hat fits, and secure with a knot.

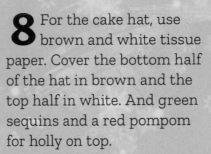

8 For the cake hat, use brown and white tissue paper. Cover the bottom half of the hat in brown and the top half in white. And green sequins and a red pompom for holly on top.

7 For the candy cane hat, use white and red tissue paper and position your fringing so it goes diagonally up and around the hat. Twist red and white pipe cleaners together and bend the top round. Poke into the top of the hat.

Paint-splattered Crackers

You can decorate these crackers to fit your Christmas theme or personalize them for each guest. In preparation for this craft, buy cracker snaps that make a bang when you pull them apart, get stocked up on little gifts that will fit inside, and start writing your jokes or riddles.

You will need

- 1 sheet of thin white card per cracker, 9 x 12in (23 x 30cm)
- Scissors
- Paint and paintbrush
- 1 sheet of tissue paper per cracker
- Double-sided tape

- 1 cardboard tube per cracker
- Ribbon
- Cracker snaps
- Adhesive tape
- Embellishments, such as pompoms, bells, ribbons, and rickrack

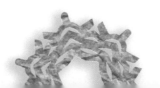

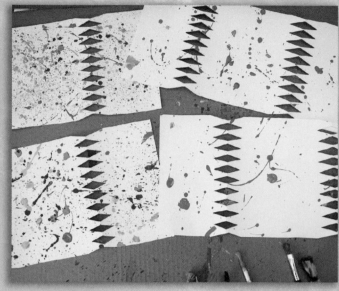

1 Use the templates (see page 142) to cut out the crackers. To make it easier to cut the diamond parts out, fold each end in half toward the middle (folding the diamonds in half) and cut them out. Cut out as many as you require to make a set of crackers.

2 Decorate the crackers. To make the paint-splatter effect, cover your work surfaces (and yourself!) and water down the paint slightly. Dip a paintbrush in the paint and flick onto the card. Leave to dry.

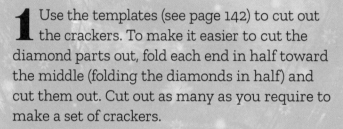

3 While the paint dries, make the paper hats. Cut a strip of tissue paper to 24 x 4in (60 x 10cm). Add double-sided tape down one of the short sides and connect the other end to form a ring shape.

4 Fold the hat into thirds and cut one end into a point.

5 Open the tissue paper back out to reveal the hat.

6 Add a line of double-sided tape on the back of the cracker along one of the long edges. Place the cardboard tube inside and roll the cracker around the tube. Seal with more double-sided tape.

7 Twist one end of each cracker to close it and tie with ribbon to secure. Slide the cracker snap into the cracker making sure it pokes out the other tied end. Tape in place at that end.

8 Slide the hat, along with a joke and gift, inside the cracker. Close the end of the cracker as before.

9 Tie the end with ribbon to secure and tape the cracker snap in place. Tie on bells and add decoration such as pompoms and rickrack to embellish.

Clay Table Set

Air-dry clay is a fantastic budget-friendly alternative to the real thing, and it can be sturdier than you might expect. This super-easy set of six place holders and napkin rings will add festive charm to any dinner table.

You will need

- 2lb (1kg) air-dry clay
- Rolling pin
- Small (about 2in/5cm) triangular cookie cutter (optional)
- Sharp knife
- Small star cookie cutter (about 1in/2.5cm)
- Acrylic paint in a range of colors, mainly green, red, and gold
- Paintbrush
- Craft glue
- Craft varnish

Tip

The possibilities for clay Christmas crafts are endless. Why not make some matching tea light holders to go with the set?

George

1 For the tree place holders, roll 10oz (300g) clay out to ¾in (2cm) thick. Use a triangular cookie cutter to cut the place holders from the clay. If you don't have a triangular cookie cutter, use a sharp knife to cut triangles from the clay.

2 Stand the triangles up on their sides, then smooth them all over with a little water.

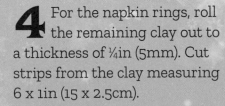

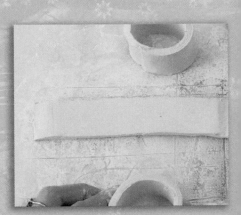

3 Ask an adult to use a sharp knife to make a slit in the top of the triangles, about ½in (1cm) deep. Wiggle the knife so that the slit opens up a little so you will be able to fit a piece of card in it. Set aside.

4 For the napkin rings, roll the remaining clay out to a thickness of ¼in (5mm). Cut strips from the clay measuring 6 x 1in (15 x 2.5cm).

5 Press down the very ends of the strips so that they taper. Then roll up the strips to form an oval shape. Pinch the ends together, then smooth with water using your fingers.

6 Ball together the remaining clay and roll it out thinly. Use the star cutter to cut six small stars. Leave all the clay overnight to dry.

7 Paint the napkin rings red, the stars gold, and the trees green. You may need a few coats to get good coverage.

8 Use the back of a paintbrush to add dots of paint to the trees.

9 Glue a star onto each napkin ring. Finish by adding a slick of varnish to each piece. This adds strength and more resistance to liquids.

Santa-spotter Binoculars

These binoculars are perfect for Santa spotting on Christmas Eve. They are easy and speedy to make from cardboard tubes and you can then decorate them with whatever you have to hand. We've used pompoms and rickrack, but you could also use ribbon, sequins, gems, felt scraps, or even tinsel!

You will need

- 3 cardboard tubes (about 5in/12cm long)
- Scissors
- Craft glue
- Paint in festive colors and paintbrushes
- Pompoms and rickrack to decorate
- Ribbon
- 2 brad paper fasteners

1 Cut one of the tubes in half across the middle and discard one of the halves.

2 Squash and fold the half tube into an hourglass shape.

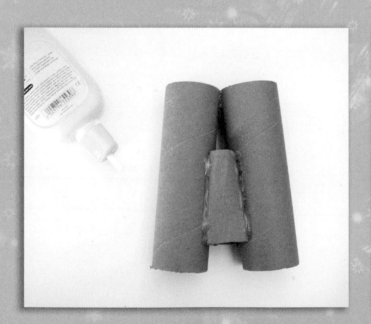

3 Glue the short tube between the two remaining tubes, roughly ½in (1cm) from one end. At the other end add a dab of glue and press the two tubes together.

4 Paint the binoculars in bright festive colors and leave to dry. You may need a few coats to get an even coverage.

5 Decorate your tubes however you like. These ones have been embellished with pompoms and rickrack.

6 Use a pair of scissors to make a small hole ½in (1cm) down from the top on each of the outer sides of the tubes at the narrower end of the binoculars. Push the brad pin through the hole, then pop the ribbon onto the point and open it out to secure.

7 Repeat on the other side and get Santa spotting.

Cardboard Toy Sleigh

This cardboard-box sleigh is a great way to keep busy while you're waiting

for Santa to arrive. Please note that the materials needed for this project

will vary depending on the size of your box and the size of your soft toy.

For the Sleigh
You will need

- Cardboard shoe box
- Pencil
- Scissors
- Gold paint and paintbrush
- 4 sheets of red card, 9 x 12in (23 x 30cm)
- Craft glue
- Gold and silver pens
- 2 sheets of silver card, 9 x 12in (23 x 30cm)
- A handful of pompoms in festive colors

For the Toy's Outfit
You will need (our one is 10in/25cm tall)

- 2 sheets of red felt, 9 x 12in (23 x 30cm)
- 1 sheet each of white and brown felt, 9 x 12in (23 x 30cm)
- About 1yd (1m) of white ribbon (about ¼in/5mm wide)
- Scissors
- Craft glue
- Large white pompom

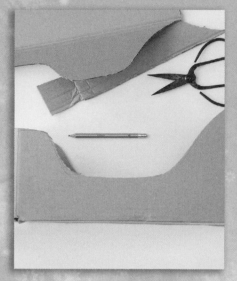

1 Sketch out the shape of a sleigh on the long side of a cardboard box. Cut this out and use the offcut as a template to cut the same shape on the other side of the box.

2 Paint the inside of the box gold and leave to dry.

3 Draw around all sides of the box on red card. Cut out and glue the card in place to cover the whole of the outside of the sleigh.

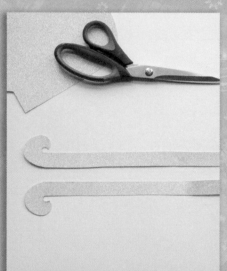

4 Use gold and silver pens to decorate the outside of the box with colorful swirls and icicles. Using the templates (see page 141) cut out two large and two small runner ends from silver card. Use the pieces to cut out mirror images of themselves.

5 Glue the eight runner-ends together in pairs so both sides are silver. Cut two strips of silver card each the same depth as the runner ends and long enough to join a small and large end, with about ½in (1cm) sticking out beyond the box at either end.

6 Glue the runners to the bottom of the sleigh, with the wide end at the back.

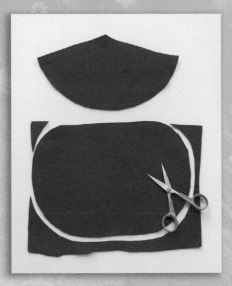

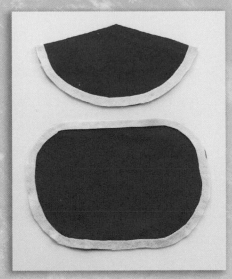

7 Decorate the top edges of the sleigh by gluing on pompoms in festive colors.

8 For a toy's cape, take a sheet of red felt and round the edges off with scissors. For the hat, draw a third of the way around a plate on the other piece of felt and cut out.

9 For the trim, trace around the cape onto white felt. Cut out, then cut the middle out, leaving a ½in (1cm) border. Repeat for the hat. Glue the trim around the hat and cape.

10 On the inside of the cape, glue a 25in (65cm) length of ribbon along one long edge and a little way around the curved edges.

11 Wrap the hat into a cone shape. Test it on your toy to fit then glue together. Fold the hat over and glue a white pompom onto the end.

12 Cut a 12 x 6in (30cm x 15cm) strip of brown felt. Fold in half and glue the sides together. Leave to dry, then turn the other way out. Cut out white felt stars and glue on. Fill with toys (or pompoms) and tie with a 10in (25cm) length of ribbon.

Pompom Stocking

There is a lot of flexibility with this project. You may want to appliqué different shapes onto the pocket for each family member or embroider names onto the cuff. Pick and choose the colors you prefer for your wool and embroidery thread. The interfacing adds a little structure to the finished stocking, so that it retains its shape when hanging, but you could leave this out if you prefer a softer look.

You will need

- 20 x 23in (50 x 60cm) red corduroy fabric
- 20 x 23in (50 x 60cm) fusible interfacing
- 18in (45cm) square white corduroy
- Scissors
- Adhesive tape
- Scrap of gray felt
- Embroidery thread and needle
- Oddments of yarn
- 10cm (25cm) white ribbon
- White thread and needle
- Iron
- Sewing pins

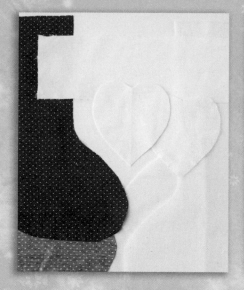

1 Fold the main fabric and interfacing in half. Place one on top of the other. Use the templates (see page 143) to cut out two stockings and two interfaces. Cut two hearts and one cuff from white corduroy.

2 Pin the interfacing pieces together and trim roughly ½in (1cm) all the way around. This will reduce bulk when you sew the stocking together.

3 Cut a star shape (see page 142) from gray felt and pin to the middle of one of the hearts. Stitch in place as shown in the photo.

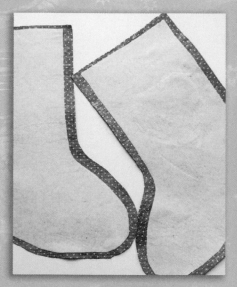

4 Place the heart pocket pieces right sides together and sew all the way around, leaving a 2in (5cm) gap along one side for turning. Make snips all the way around the excess fabric to prevent puckering.

5 Turn the pocket the right way out and press with an iron, tucking in the raw edge from the gap. Pin the pocket centrally onto one of the stocking pieces, about 4in (10cm) from the top. Sew in place leaving the top open.

6 Follow the maker's guidelines to fuse the interface to the back of the stocking pieces. Pin the two stocking pieces right sides together and sew all the way around, leaving the top open. Turn out and press.

7 Cut a cuff from white corduroy, 4 x 19in (10 x 48cm). Wrap around the stocking, right sides together. Pin the ends together so it fits snugly. Remove and sew the cuff together where pinned.

8 Press the two sides of the white cuff under by ½in (1cm) to conceal the raw edges. Sew all the way along one of the folds, with a small seam allowance.

9 Place the cuff inside the stocking, wrong sides together, with the sewn side of the cuff sticking out of the top of the stocking by 2½in (6cm). Pin then sew all around the stocking just along the fold.

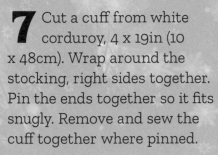

10 Fold the cuff down over the stocking. To add a monogram, mark out in pencil an initial or name on the cuff and back stitch it in place using embroidery thread (see page 58).

11 Now make pompoms. For a large one, wind yarn around your hand about 100 times. Peel away and tie with yarn in the middle, as tightly as you can. Snip through all the loops and trim. For smaller pompoms, wrap the yarn about 60 times.

12 For the hanging loop, fold the ribbon in half and sew it inside the stocking. Hand stitch the pompoms onto the top corner of the stocking using white thread.

Christmas Eve Box

This is the ultimate festive treat to make Christmas Eve extra special. Fill it with loads of treats to get kids in the festive spirit. We've used festive shapes for the box but you can personalize it with the recipient's name.

For the Festive Box
You will need

- Strong cardboard or wooden box (ours measures 10in/25cm square)
- Red paint and paintbrush
- Felt in a variety of colors
- Scissors
- Craft glue
- Embellishments such as mini pompoms, rickrack, sequins, or buttons

1 Begin by painting your box red inside and out. You may need a few coats to get an even coverage.

2 Use the templates (see page 142) to cut festive shapes out of felt or make your own design.

3 Embellish the festive felt shapes by gluing on mini pompoms, rickrack, sequins, and buttons.

4 Glue the felt shapes onto the outside of the box and the lid. Add some mini pompoms, then glue rickrack trim around the edge of the lid.

For the Reindeer Food
You will need

- A few handfuls of oats
- A handful of dried fruit
- Sprinkles
- Sheet of brown paper at least 7in (18cm) square

- Glue stick
- 2 googly eyes
- Red pompom
- Black pen
- 2 brown pipe cleaners
- Adhesive tape

1 Mix the oats, dried fruit, and sprinkles together in a bowl.

2 To make the envelope, cut a 7in (18cm) square of brown paper. Fold in half diagonally, then open out and repeat folding and reopening in the other direction.

3 Fold two opposite corners into the middle.

4 Glue the edges of one of the other corners, fold up to the middle, and stick to the sides. Fold the top corner down to the middle. Leave unglued for now.

5 Glue the googly eyes and pompom onto the front to make a face. Add a little smile in pen.

6 Bend two pipe cleaners into antlers. Tape them inside the top corners of the envelope. Fill with the reindeer food and seal with glue.

Tasty Christmas Treats

These lovely little bakes are easy to make with kids and taste absolutely delicious. They are the perfect addition to a Christmas tea party or to leave out as a delicious treat for Santa on Christmas Eve.

For the Mini Christmas Cake Truffles
You will need (makes 12–14)

- 2 Graham crackers (digestive biscuits)
- 6oz (180g) milk chocolate
- ¼ stick (25g) butter
- ⅓ cup (70ml) heavy (double) cream

- 1oz (20g) green fondant icing
- Rolling pin
- Red sugar pearls
- Truffle paper liners (cases)

1 Place the crackers onto a plate and, with clean fingers, squash them until they are crumbs. Break up 5oz (150g) of chocolate into a bowl with the butter and cream. Microwave in short bursts, stirring frequently until it has all melted and combined.

2 Add the crumbs to the chocolate mixture and stir well. Refrigerate for at least 4 hours until set.

3 Finely grate the remaining chocolate onto a plate. Use a teaspoon to scoop out the mixture, then form it into balls with your hands. Roll the balls in the grated chocolate.

4 Thinly roll out some green fondant and cut tiny diamond shapes. Place them on the truffles and push a red sugar pearl into each one. Place into a paper liner to finish.

For the Pinwheel Cookies
You will need (makes 16)

- 2 sticks (220g) butter
- 1⅓ cups (270g) superfine (caster) sugar
- 2 eggs
- 3 cups (370g) plain flour
- ½ tsp baking powder
- Red and green food color gel
- Plastic wrap (cling film)
- Parchment paper

1 Beat the butter and sugar in a mixer until creamy. Beat in the eggs gradually, then beat in the flour. Divide the mixture into three. Wrap one piece in plastic wrap and shape roughly into a rectangle.

2 Place a portion in the bowl. Add a few drops of green food coloring and beat until mixed. Clean the bowl then repeat to make a portion red. Wrap each in plastic wrap and refrigerate all for an hour.

3 Roll each dough out between sheets of plastic wrap, to ¼in (5mm) thick. Remove the wrap from the top of each one. Stack them using the wrap on the bottom to pick each up and flip it over.

4 Roll the dough together a little. Remove the top wrap and use the bottom wrap to roll the dough into a large sausage roughly 2½in (6cm) in diameter. Cover in plastic wrap and refrigerate overnight.

5 Preheat the oven to 350°F (180°C). Remove the plastic wrap and chop the dough into rounds, ½in (1cm) thick.

6 Place the cookies on a baking sheet lined with parchment paper and bake for 12-15 minutes. Cool on a wire rack.

For the Crunchy Snowmen
You will need (makes 10-12)

- Parchment paper
- 3 cups (80g) crispy rice cereal, such as Rice Krispies
- ½ cup (50g) desiccated coconut
- 1¼ cups (75g) mini white marshmallows

- 14oz (400g) white chocolate
- 2 small round cookie cutters (different sizes)
- 20-24 chocolate chips
- Black writing icing
- 1oz (30g) each of red and green fondant icing

1 Lay out a sheet of parchment paper on a baking sheet. Place the cereal, coconut, and marshmallows into a large bowl. Break the chocolate into chunks in another bowl and microwave it in short blasts until melted. Pour the chocolate over the dry ingredients and stir.

2 Use a teaspoon to add dollops of the mixture into the larger cookie cutter on the parchment paper, to make the body of the snowman. Remove the cutter to leave a round of mixture. Repeat with the smaller cutter to make the heads. Remove the cutter then push the shapes together a little to make sure they are touching. Add chocolate chips to the body for buttons, then leave to set for about 2 hours.

3 Add black icing dots to the heads for eyes, then roll out the fondant nice and thin and cut long strips. Wrap around the neck for scarves.

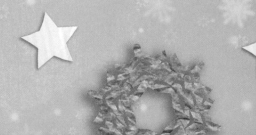

Templates

All templates need to be enlarged on a photocopier to 145%. Align the templates as near to the top left-hand corner of the photocopier glass as possible. You may need to repeat a few times to find the best position.

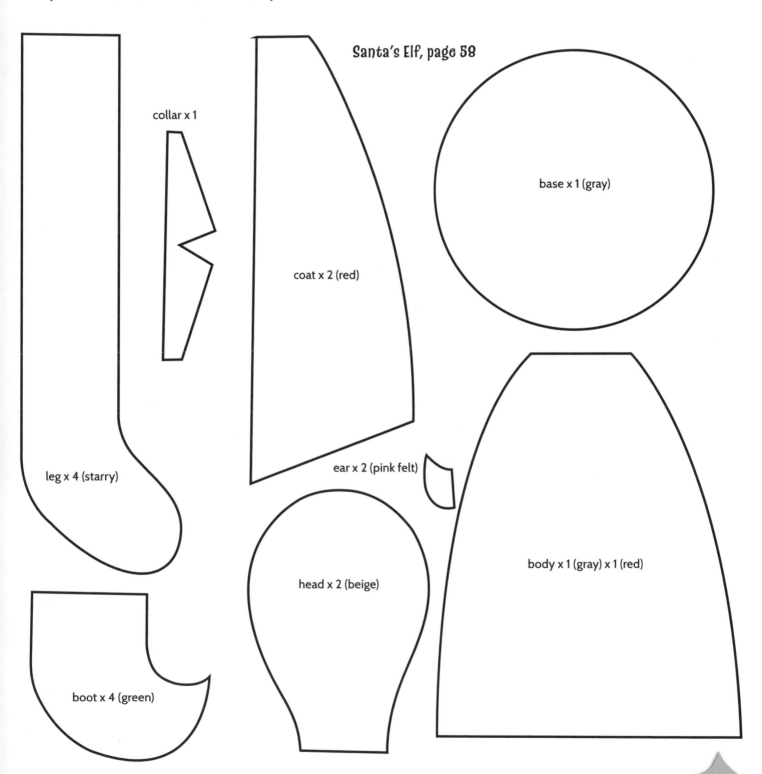

Santa's Elf, page 58

collar x 1

leg x 4 (starry)

coat x 2 (red)

base x 1 (gray)

ear x 2 (pink felt)

head x 2 (beige)

body x 1 (gray) x 1 (red)

boot x 4 (green)

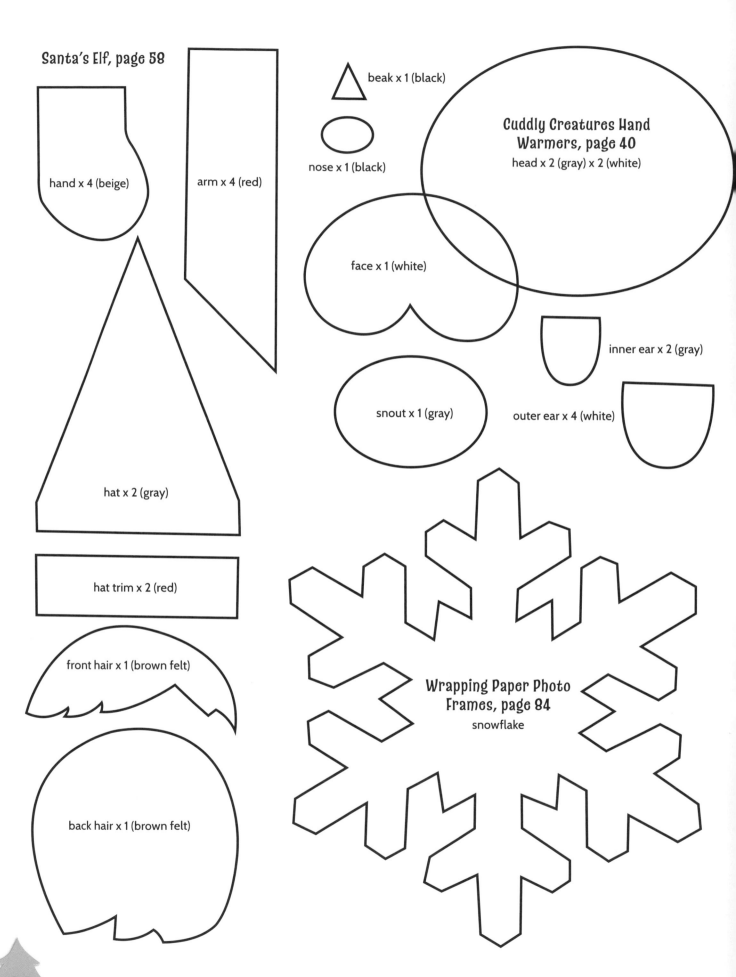

Santa's Elf, page 58

hand x 4 (beige)

arm x 4 (red)

beak x 1 (black)

nose x 1 (black)

Cuddly Creatures Hand Warmers, page 40
head x 2 (gray) x 2 (white)

face x 1 (white)

inner ear x 2 (gray)

hat x 2 (gray)

snout x 1 (gray)

outer ear x 4 (white)

hat trim x 2 (red)

front hair x 1 (brown felt)

Wrapping Paper Photo Frames, page 84

snowflake

back hair x 1 (brown felt)

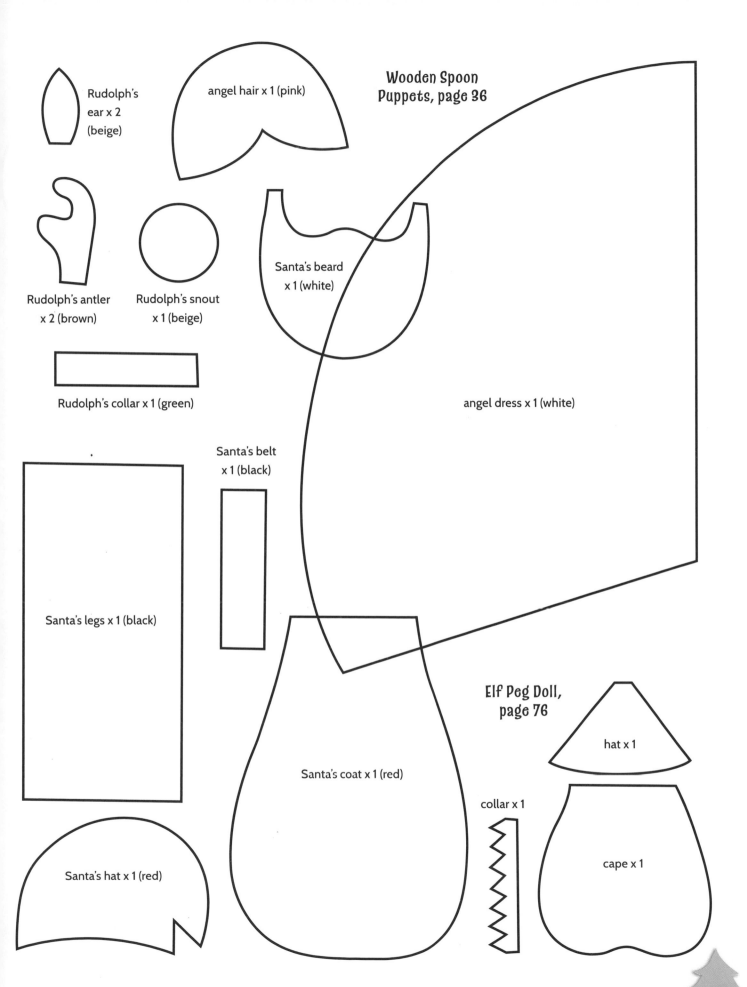

Rudolph's ear x 2 (beige)

angel hair x 1 (pink)

Wooden Spoon Puppets, page 36

Rudolph's antler x 2 (brown)

Rudolph's snout x 1 (beige)

Santa's beard x 1 (white)

Rudolph's collar x 1 (green)

angel dress x 1 (white)

Santa's belt x 1 (black)

Santa's legs x 1 (black)

Elf Peg Doll, page 76

hat x 1

Santa's coat x 1 (red)

collar x 1

Santa's hat x 1 (red)

cape x 1

139

Nutcracker Skittles, page 54

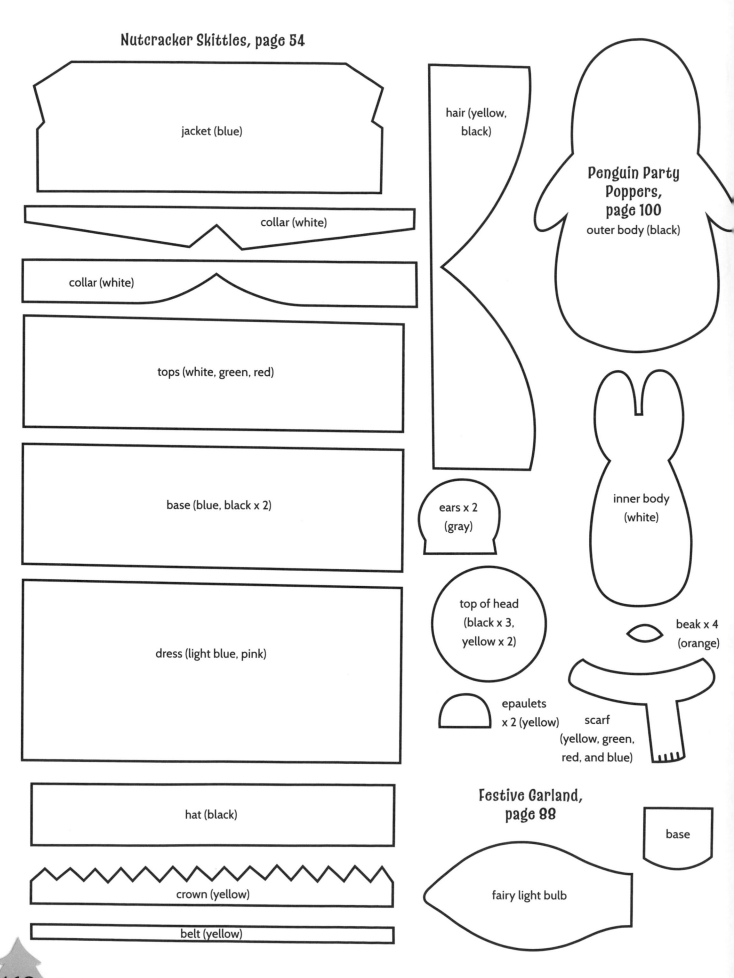

jacket (blue)

hair (yellow, black)

Penguin Party Poppers, page 100

outer body (black)

collar (white)

collar (white)

tops (white, green, red)

inner body (white)

ears x 2 (gray)

base (blue, black x 2)

top of head (black x 3, yellow x 2)

beak x 4 (orange)

dress (light blue, pink)

epaulets x 2 (yellow)

scarf (yellow, green, red, and blue)

Festive Garland, page 88

hat (black)

base

crown (yellow)

fairy light bulb

belt (yellow)

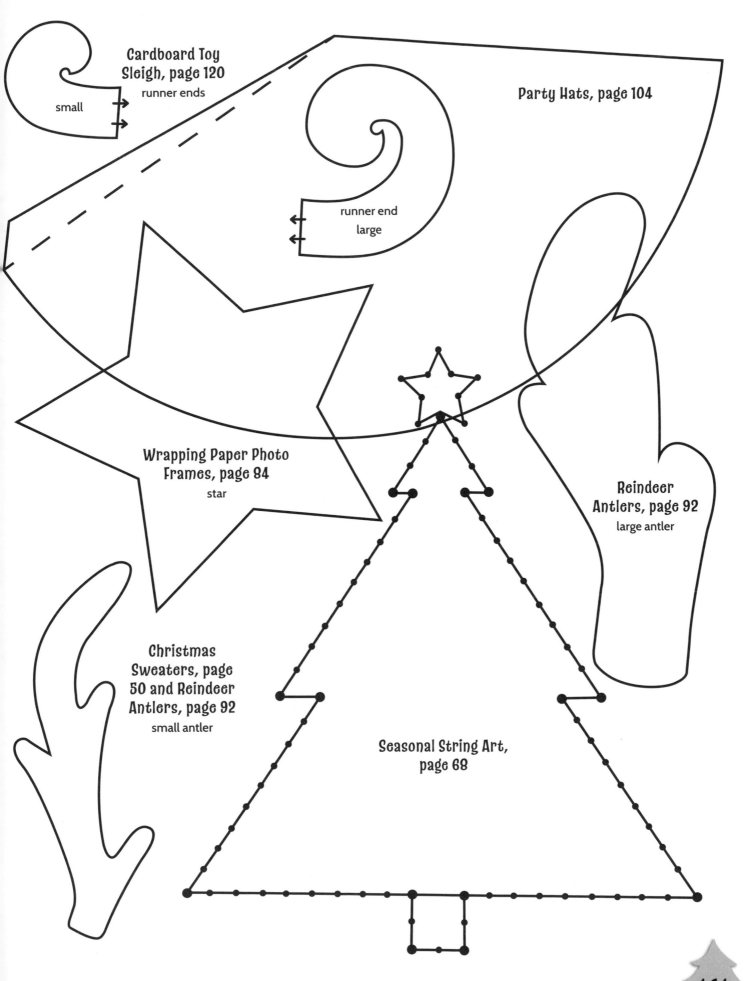

Cardboard Toy
Sleigh, page 120

runner ends

small

Party Hats, page 104

runner end
large

Wrapping Paper Photo
Frames, page 84

star

Reindeer
Antlers, page 92

large antler

Christmas
Sweaters, page
50 and Reindeer
Antlers, page 92

small antler

Seasonal String Art,
page 68

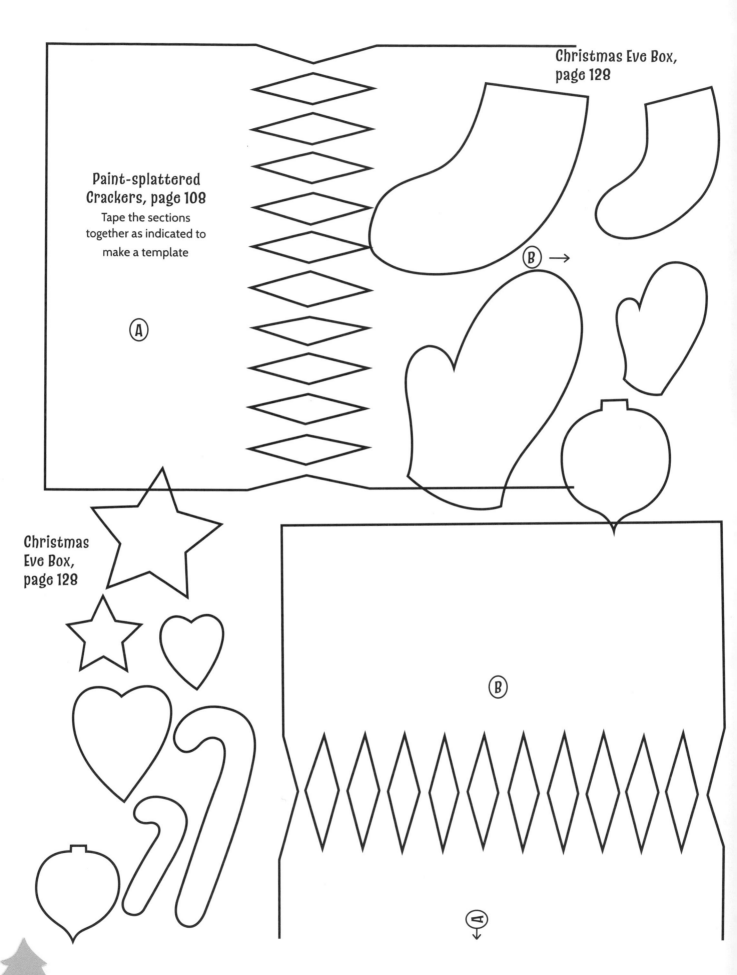

Christmas Eve Box, page 128

Paint-splattered Crackers, page 108

Tape the sections together as indicated to make a template

Ⓐ

Ⓑ →

Christmas Eve Box, page 128

Ⓑ

Ⓐ

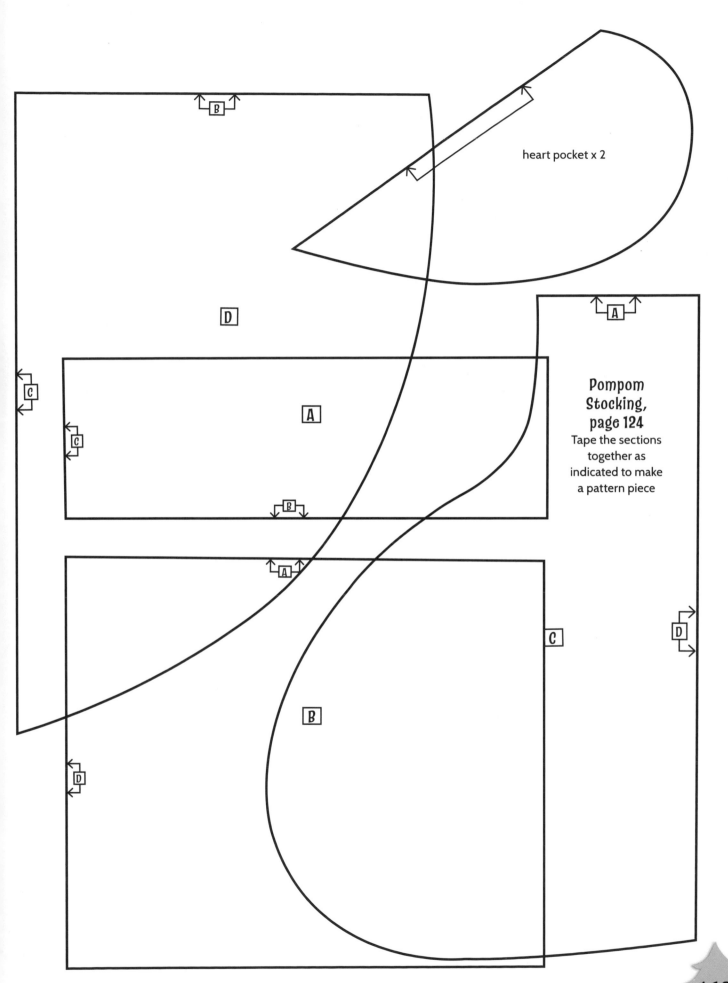

heart pocket x 2

D

B

C

C

A

B

A

Pompom Stocking, page 124
Tape the sections together as indicated to make a pattern piece

C

D

B

D

About the Authors

Laura Minter and Tia Williams are crafters, mothers, and writers. They started Little Button Diaries, their award-winning craft blog, in 2014 to show that having children doesn't mean you have to stop doing the things you love. There is always time for crafting (as well as tea and cookies)! They have written many craft books and created projects for major retailers Hobbycraft, Paperchase, Brother Sewing, and Duck Tape. Between them, they have five children who they love making things for (and with!).

Follow them at:
Twitter: @LButtondiaries
Instagram: @littlebuttondiaries
Tag your photos: #christmascraftbook

Acknowledgments

GMC Publications would like to thank our lovely models Cressida, Grayson, Harper, Ivy, Kiki, Nancy, William, and Marnie.

The publishers and authors can accept no legal responsibility for any consequences arising from the application of information, advice, or instructions given in this publication.

A catalog record for this book is available from the British Library.

Publisher: **Jonathan Bailey**
Production: **Jim Bulley, Jon Hoag**
Senior Project Editor: **Wendy McAngus**
Designer: **Cathy Challinor**
Stylist: **Anna Stevens**

Color origination by GMC Reprographics.
Printed and bound in China

Main photography by Andrew Perris, step-by-step photography by Laura Minter and Tia Williams. Other photographs Shutterstock.com

First published 2021 by Guild of Master Craftsman Publications Ltd, Castle Place, 166 High Street, Lewes, East Sussex, BN7 1XU, UK.

Text © Laura Minter and Tia Williams, 2021. Copyright in the Work © GMC Publications Ltd, 2021.

ISBN 978 1 78494 623 4

 For more information contact: GMC Publications Ltd, Castle Place, 166 High Street, Lewes, East Sussex, BN7 1XU, United Kingdom
Tel: +44 (0)1273 488005 gmcbooks.com